# The Right to Bear Arms in a Modern America

Can the Second Amendment
& Our Modern World Coexist?

What was the original intent of the right to a regulated Militia
& the right of the people to keep and bear arms?

How have Supreme Court Decisions
Defined the Second Amendment?

# Amendment II

"A well regulated Militia, being necessary to the security of a free State, the right of the people to keep and bear Arms, shall not be infringed."

# Contents

# Introduction

The original Constitution, which 39 state delegates signed on September 17, 1787, after a four-month long Constitutional Convention, made it clear that any newly formed Federal Government of the United State of America would have limited powers.

While the original Constitution expressed the notion of limited power within the Federal Government, it provided few specific rights and liberties for the people. Without these individual rights attached to the Constitution, many state delegates believed that a strong Federal Government could potentially abuse its citizens by denying them basic rights.

These delegates, called Anti-Federalists, were led by Virginia's Patrick Henry, who did not sign the original Constitution and demanded a Bill of Rights for the people, refusing to support ratification of the document without amendments attached to it. Reluctantly, the Federalists led by Virginia delegate James Madison, the Father of the Constitution, being its primary writer, and New York delegate Alexander Hamilton agreed to the amendments in order to complete ratification.

The Federal Government of the United States under the U.S. Constitution began operation on March 4, 1789, and on September 25, 1789, the first Congress adopted 12 amendments to the Constitution. In 1791, the states ratified 10 of those amendments.

Sharing the Second Amendment of the 10 amendments are two ideas that the framers of the Constitution constructed to align with one another, although the specific reason for the alignment is not altogether clear in the eyes of many. The ambiguity of their relationship to one another has created division in the years since ratification. Additionally, the American populace has tested both ideas as separate entities through the years because of the amendments simple phrasing and lack of elaboration. Therefore, interpretations of the amendment are vast, and its place within the context of today's society adds to the complexity of the 27 words that make up Amendment II, which read:

"A well regulated Militia, being necessary to the security of a free State, the right of the people to keep and bear Arms, shall not be infringed."

The U.S. Constitution is the world's longest surviving written charter of government, according to multiple sources, including the National Archives and the Encyclopedia Britannica. It is a miracle of invention, considering that the average lifespan of a national constitution is 17 years since 1789, according to University of Chicago law and political science professor Thomas Ginsburg.

While the U.S. Constitution is brilliant, do all of its 18th-Century notions make sense in a modern world? Specifically, should the right to keep and bear arms apply to today's relentlessly violent society where mentally and emotional disturbed individuals make headlines everyday by killing people in mass with high-powered , modernized weaponry?

In an objective way, we explore the original application of the Second Amendment, as well as how the United State's courts have defined it through the years.

# Supreme Court Decisions Attempt to Define the Second Amendment

Because of the age of the U.S. Constitution, it seems reasonable to test it. Consider that since its ratification, the U.S. has expanded by 37 states from the original 13, and the population of the nation has increased by more than 320 million citizens.

In particular, the Second Amendment must wade through conscientious waters as the technology of weaponry has advance considerably since the creation of the Second Amendment, moving from muskets to machine guns. In all, the Supreme Court has tested the interpretation of the Second Amendment on seven occasions.

United States v. Cruikshank

We find the first test in the case *United States v. Cruikshank* (1875), which involved the use of a firearm, deemed illegal, during the murder of more than a hundred black men over a political dispute. The overall decision by the Court was complex and convoluted, but one part of the decision was clear, which is that the Second Amendment does not prohibit state and municipal regulation of firearms. The Court issued the following: "The Second Amendment declares that it shall not be infringed; but this, as has been seen, means no more than that it shall not be infringed by Congress. This is one of the amendments that has no other effect than to restrict the powers of the national government."

# Presser v. Illinois

In *Presser v. Illinois* (1886), The Supreme Court reiterated the stance found in *United States v. Cruikshank*, by applying it to state regulation, stating the following: "The provision in the Second Amendment to the Constitution, that 'The right of the people to keep and bear arms shall not be infringed' is a limitation only on the power of Congress and the national government, and not of the states."

In this case, the Supreme Court also clarified notions involving a well-regulated militia by disposing of the argument that individuals have the right to assemble as a militia independent of state or federal authorization by issuing the following statement: "It shall not be lawful for any body of men whatever other than the regular organized volunteer militia of this state and the troops of the United States to associate themselves together as a military company or organization, or to drill or parade with arms in any city or town of this state without the license of the Governor thereof."

# Miller v. Texas

*Miller v. Texas* (1894) was an elaborate case involving the murder of a police officer with an unlicensed handgun. In the proceedings, Franklin Miller questioned the validity of a Texas gun restriction law, saying it violated the Fourteenth Amendment, which states: "No state shall make or enforce any law which shall abridge the privileges or immunities of citizens of the United States; nor shall any state deprive any person of life, liberty, or property, without due process of law; nor deny to any person within its jurisdiction the equal protection of the laws."

The addition of the Fourteenth Amendment into the fold of individual rights, which Congress ratified in 1868, either further complicates the voice of the Second Amendment, or clarifies its message by making it harder for states to regulate, restrict, or "infringe upon" gun ownership. However, in this case, regardless of the Fourteenth Amendment, the Supreme Court again ruled that the Second Amendment did not apply to state laws, in this case, Texas laws.

# United States v. Miller

In *United States v. Miller* (1939), the Supreme Court tied the Second Amendment's two ideas, Militia and Arms, together for the first time in a dispute over the transportation of an unregistered sawed-off shotgun across states lines, which violated the National Firearms Act of 1934 that regulated short-barreled rifles, machineguns, and silencers. The court ruled that the Second Amendment did not protect the charged man because his act did not assist in the cause of a state Militia or the defense of the United States, stating the following:

"In the absence of any evidence tending to show that possession or use of a 'shotgun having a barrel of less than eighteen inches in length' at this time has some reasonable relationship to the preservation or efficiency of a well regulated Militia, we cannot say that the Second Amendment guarantees the right to keep and bear such an instrument. Certainly it is not within judicial notice that this weapon is any part of the ordinary military equipment or that its use could contribute to the common defense."

## Lewis v. United States

In *Lewis v. United States* (1980), which had no direct link to the Second Amendment, discussed the merits of the Gun Control Act of 1968 as well as other laws that prohibited felons from owning a firearm. The Supreme Court said the following about gun control laws: "These legislative restrictions on the use of firearms are neither based upon constitutionally suspect criteria, nor do they trench upon any constitutionally protected liberties."

Afterwards, the Court called upon statements found in *United States v. Miller* to conclude the Court's point, saying that the Second Amendment guarantees no right to keep and bear a firearm that does not have some reasonable relationship to the preservation or efficiency of a well-regulated Militia.

# Two Supreme Court Decisions
# Change the Rules Regarding State Gun Control

# District of Columbia v. Heller

In 2008, a case reached the Supreme Court docket that dismantled previous court case's claims that while Congress could not infringe upon the right to bear arms, states did have the power to regulate and restrict gun ownership. The Fourteenth Amendment did a lot to further the individual rights of America citizens while simultaneously stripping states of their autonomy from the proscriptions imposed upon Congress that are found in the Constitution and its Amendments. *District of Columbia v. Heller* (2008) made it clear that states had little say in the direction of modern gun policy. The case also reversed the ideas found in previous Supreme Court decisions that the Constitution intentionally aligned and attached "the right to keep and bear Arms" with the "right to maintain a well-regulated state Militia".

The complaint began after Dick Heller, a District of Columbia special police officer authorized to carry a handgun while performing his duties at the Federal Judicial Center, attempted to register a personal handgun that he intended to keep at his D.C. home. The District of Columbia denied his request under a provision found in D.C.'s Firearms Control Act of 1975.

Heller took the case to court, claiming that two provisions in the Firearms Control Act violated his Constitutional rights under the Second Amendment. One of the provisions prohibited the possession of handguns, and the second one required that lawful firearms in the home be unloaded and disassembled or trigger-locked.

After Heller's case made the rounds in the lower courts, the United State Supreme Court ruled that the two local gun laws violated the Constitution. The decision had opposition, though, as the Supreme Court justices voted 5-4 in favor of Heller. While the majority of the Court ruled that the "The Second Amendment protects an individual right to possess a firearm unconnected with service in the militia," and that individuals had the right to use that firearm "for traditionally lawful purposes, such as self-defense within the home," four of the nine Justices disagreed. As one might assume, for the most part, known political ideals divided the chamber.

Two of the dissenting justices, Ruth Badar Ginsburg and Stephen Gerald Breyer were appointed by Democratic presidents. John P. Stevens and David Souter cast the other dissenting votes, and while Republic presidents appointed them, they both voted reliably with the courts liberal members. In fact, in 2003, a statistical analysis of voting patterns showed that Stevens had become the most liberal member of the court.

Those Justices siding with Heller, were all appointed by a Republican president, and included John Roberts, Samuel Alito, Clarence Thomas, Anthony Kennedy, and Antonin Scalia.

When Justice Scalia delivered his ruling opinion to the Court, which interpreted certain measures of the Second Amendment, he set out to make his reasoning clear, as it veered from previous Court decisions.

First, he said that the original delegates that ratified the Second Amendment wrote it to be understood by the voters; its words and phrases were used in a normal and ordinary way; therefore, they exclude secret or technical meanings that would not have been known to ordinary citizens in the founding generation.

Next, Scalia declared that the framers of Second Amendment divided it into two parts. The first part secures the right of the people to a well-regulated militia. The second secures the right of the people to keep and bear arms. The two do not work in unison; they are separate ideas, according toe Scalia.

The District of Columbia argued that the Second Amendment was one complete idea, stating that only members of a militia had the right to bear arms. Justice Scalia thwarted that notion even though it had Supreme Court case precedent. Scalia said that "The right of the people" refers to individual rights and belongs to all Americans.

Third, he also clarified numerous terms found in the Second Amendment in order to clarify the phrase "keep and bear Arms":

- According to two popular dictionaries of the era in which the delegates created the Constitution, "keep" meant "to retain, not to lose," and "to have in custody," as well as "to hold; to retain in one's power or possession."

- The dictionaries defined "bear" to mean "carry."

- The word "Arms" meant "weapons of offence, or armor of defence" and "anything that man wears for his defence, or takes into his hands, or useth in wrath to cast at or strike another,". Therefore, the term "Arms" is not specific to military use.

Therefore, "keep and bear arms" means to "have weapons in custody and carry for offence."

Finally, Scalia explained that just as modern forms of communication are included in the First Amendment, and modern forms of search are included in the Fourth Amendment, the Second Amendment extends "arms" to include all instruments that constitute modern forms of bearable arms, even those not in existence when the country's Founding Fathers created the Amendment.

## McDonald v. City of Chicago

In *McDonald v. City of Chicago* (2010), the Supreme Court found another local gun restriction law to be in violation of the Constitution by a 5-4 vote. Again, a municipality banned the registration of a handgun to a law-abiding citizen, and the same *District of Columbia v. Heller* Court justices presided over the case, with the exception of newly appointed justice Sonia Sotomayor, a President Barrack Obama appointee. Again, votes fell along the lines of known political ideals of liberalism and conservatism, and the Supreme Court deemed the local law unconstitutional.

# Dissenting Opinions on the Individual Right to Keep & Bear Arms

The dissenting opinion in the *District of Columbia v. Heller* decision came from Stevens and Breyer. Stevens said that the Second Amendment creators never meant to protect an individual's rights to keep and bear arms outside of the context of military service, and they never intended to limit the government's authority to regulate civilian use or possession of firearms. Stevens called the majority decision "strained and unpersuasive" as well as "overwrought and novel."

Breyer took a different approach that Stevens in his dissent, contending that if the Second Amendment provides for an individual's right of self-defense as argued, that municipalities in urban areas where gun crime and gun violence are extensive should be able to regulate firearm possession to protect individuals. Therefore, gun control laws can be consistent with Second Amendment rights if the Constitutional provision's intent is to provide citizens a measure of "self-defense".

Similar dissenting opinions by Stevens and Breyer followed the *McDonald v. City of Chicago* decision, and their opinions use key evidence found in the manuscripts of James Madison to validate their points.

Justice Stevens places significance on James Madison's inclusion of a conscientious-objector clause in an early draft of the Second Amendment, which delegates later removed. Madison writes, "but no person religiously scrupulous of bearing arms, shall be compelled to render military service in person," and Stevens argues that the phrasing and the idea by Madison establishes that the meaning of "bear Arms" refers only to military service.

There is more evidence to be found along these lines, evidence found in the journey that brought the Second Amendment to the citizens of the newly formed nation of the United States.

# Creation of the Bill of Rights
# & the Original Intent of the Second Amendment

James Madison initially wanted to incorporate the amendments to the Constitution into the text of the original document. However, other delegates disagreed with the idea, and in the end, Madison and company attached the Bill of Rights to the tail of the Constitution.

Madison and crew arranged the 10 amendments in a particular order, and many people today consider the Founding Father's high placement of the Second Amendment within the first 10 Amendments as a measure of its importance. Amendment I, people argue, is the most important of the amendments because it makes it clear that the Federal Government could not establish a national religion, and could not suppress the right to free speech, the right to a free press, the right to peaceful assembly, or the right to petition the Government.

Right after it, we find Amendment II, appearing to many as a continued narrative on individual rights. However, there is more evidence that shows that the delegates ordered the amendments according to how they would naturally fit within the existing composition of the Constitution; and not ordered by perceived importance.

For example, the First Amendment relates to the powers of the legislature, and begins with "Congress shall make no law", so its placement would naturally occur *after* Article I, Section 8, which begins with "Congress shall have power," and within Article I, Section 9, which is a list of proscriptions. Because the Second, Third, and Fourth Amendment also limit what Congress has the power to do, they would also fall into Article I.

Article II of the Constitution moves onto executive power, but there are no amendments within the Bill of Rights that pertain to the executive branch. Article III of the Constitution establishes the court system, so Amendments Five through Eight fall into that section because they deal with juries, bail, and cruel and unusual punishments. Amendments Nine and Ten would be a postscript to the Constitution because they deal with the interpretation of the Constitution and the other amendments in their entirety.

The conundrum is how the Second Amendment slides between the two ideas found in the First and Third Amendments. The First Amendment clearly deals with the individual rights of the people to particular freedoms that include religion, speech, press, assembly, and government petition. The Third Amendment deals with power of Congress during war, providing that Congress could not quarter soldiers in the homes of citizens. In the middle, we have the Second Amendment that discusses a militia like those found in Lexington and Concord where the first battle of the Revolutionary War began.

The colonial militias were autonomous groups that self-trained in weapons, tactics, and strategy several times each year, and were responsive to threats against their territory from any enemy that might venture into their town. That threat eventually became the British Redcoats, and the militias held their own during the prologue of war as the Continental Army formed to coordinate the military efforts of all the colonies during the Revolutionary War.

The importance of the militia to those early American delegates is obvious. Before the Continental Army organized to a full realization under George Washington, the only line of defense in colonial America was the individual militia groups that dotted the landscape.

Coming back to the Second Amendment, the question for some becomes, why is the idea of "a well regulated Militia" coupled with "the right of the people to keep and bear Arms." The argument for those in the "gun control" quarters is that if the right to bear arms is an individual right, it would be found in the First Amendment where individual rights are targeted in a clear and meaningful way. Instead, Madison and his men placed the right to bear arms *after* those First Amendment rights and coupled it with the delegate's stance on militias.

## The National Guard and State Militias

There are many who debate the meaning behind the right of each state to maintain a well-regulated militia, but no one has ever tested its definitions in a real way at the Supreme Court level. For the most part, citizens understand that each state's National Guard provides for this nation's militias. Some disagree, but the National Guard and the United States Government do not.

The National Guard takes the stance that the "first militia regiments in North America were organized in Massachusetts. Based upon an order of the Massachusetts Bay Colony's General Court, the colony's militia was organized into three permanent regiments to better defend the colony."

Today, the descendents of these first regiments make up the 181st Infantry, the 182nd Infantry, the 101st Field Artillery, and the 101st Engineer Battalion of the Massachusetts National Guard.

The National Guard stance continues: "December 13, 1626, thus marks the beginning of the organized militia, and the birth of the National Guard's oldest organized units is symbolic of the founding of all the state, territory, and District of Columbia militias that collectively make up today's National Guard."

This United States Congress codified the notion that each state's National Guard is its militia by order of the Constitution by enacting the "Militia Act" in 1903, and subsequent acts pertaining to the National Guard over the years.

Each time the act evolves, the Federal Government takes bolder steps towards complete ownership of its identity.

Furthermore, the National Guard's roots extend way before 1903. It is found in English common law and American colonial customs, and the first Militia Act that the newly-formed United States enacted was in 1792, the year after the states ratified the Bill of Rights. From that early date, the President of the United States could call upon the militia as needed to serve the needs of the Federal Government. This Act required every able-bodied man from 18 to 45 to serve in a militia, which the state legislature would direct, and these men had to "arm" themselves with a musket or rifle at their own expense and participate in a yearly military inspection.

The Federal Government called state militias into action during the War of 1812 and the Spanish-America War in 1898. However, through the 1800s, the militia system became an unorganized and under-funded entity that required reform. The Militia Act of 1903 organized the National Guard into a component of the U.S. Military with funding provided by both the Federal and state governments, and made it clear that the U.S. Government could federalize the National Guard for national security reasons. Therefore, National Guard members recite a dual oath to the United States and their state government.

Although, to complicate matters, the Militia Act of 1903 classified the militia in two ways:

- The organized militia, which consists of the National Guard and the Naval Militia

- The unorganized militia, which consists of the members of the militia who are not members of the National Guard or the Naval Militia

The Act goes into great detail about the "organized" militia, but nothing more is said to define the "unorganized militia". Basic theory suggests that the unorganized militia pertains to able-bodied men that are not in the National Guard, Reserves, or the U.S. Military, who are subject to military conscription through the Selective Service System.

# Militias Defined within the Original Constitution

According to the Constitution and proceeding government doctrine, a militia is not a renegade bunch of gun enthusiasts keeping the Federal Government in check. No, the Militia is an armed, trained, and disciplined group of soldiers controlled by their home state or by the United States Congress in an organized or unorganized fashion. This idea is written in Article I, Section 8 of the Constitution: "The Congress shall have the power to provide for the calling forth the Militia to execute the Laws of the Union, suppress insurrections, and repel invasions."

In other words, according to the Constitution, the intent of the Militia is not to guard state powers against Federal tyranny, but to "execute the laws of the Union," and the Union as we know is the United States of America. Furthermore, the following clause in Article I, Section 8 states that Congress shall have the following power: "To provide for organizing, arming, and disciplining the Militia, and for governing such Part of them as may be employed in the Service of the United States, reserving to the States respectively, the Appointment of the Officers, and the Authority of training the Militia according to the discipline prescribed by Congress."

Therefore, it is curious that the "right bear arms" shares the same space in the Second Amendment with the right for a state militia. In an essay by James Madison titled *Federalist No. 46,* he stressed that Federal and state governments are different agencies, but are to be collaborative. However, Madison goes into detail that there will be a "regular army" that will "be entirely at the devotion of the Federal Government", but to dissuade fears of this federal force, Madison makes it knows that "the State governments, with the people on their side, would be able to repel the danger," and this is how:

"To these would be opposed a militia amounting to near half a million citizens with arms in their hands," which follows a sentence where he says specifically that "a standing army can be carried in any country, does not exceed one hundredth part of souls," which is Madison talking about the entire population of the Union while differentiating the whole of the population from its militia, saying "or, one twenty-fifth part of the number able to bear arms."

Here, he is saying "25 percent of the country" had the right to bear arms. It is believed that there were 2.5 million people living in the original 13 states in 1776, and 20 percent of the population were slaves. Therefore, the population of free citizens would have been 2 million, and 25 percent of 2 million is 500,000. Therefore, to summarize, he is saying that the militia, made up of 500,000 capable men, were able to bear arms.

Why did Madison write the Second Amendment with both the Militia and the "right to bear Arms" within the same sentence? We will never know, but there is evidence to support both the individual right to keep and bear arms, and the right of a militia, only, to keep and bear arms.

## Mischaracterized Intent of the Second Amendment

Oftentimes, the evidence to support the right to bear arms for every individual is taken out of context or parsed in ways to illuminate great falsities. A common mischaracterization by gun rights activists is a quote by Virginia delegate Patrick Henry, which states: "The great object is that every man be armed. Everyone who is able might have a gun."

Henry was a militiaman, and a staunch advocate of militias. In 1775 before delivering his famous "Give me liberty or give me death!" he gave an impassioned plea during the Second Virginia Convention that the colonies should form militias to defend themselves against the British. Henry was also one of the stars of the Virginia Ratifying Convention, along with James Madison.

The Virginia Convention was put together a year after the United States Constitution had been drafted and provided for the final ratification of the Constitution and its amendments. During the convention, the "Great Orator" as Henry was known, is talking about a militia and their need for arms in the case of the mischaracterized quote above. The full quote states:

"May we not discipline and arm them, as well as Congress if the power be concurrent? So that our militia shall have two sets of arms, double sets of regimentals, and thus, at a very great cost, we shall be doubly armed. The great object is, that every man armed. But can the people afford to pay for double sets of arms, Every one Who is able may have a gun. But we have learned, by experience, that, necessary as it is have arms, and though our

Assembly has, by a succession of laws for many years, endeavored to have the militia completely armed, is still far from being the case."

From there, a list of amendments was ratified, but work still needed to be done at the state levels. Originally the Second Amendment was the "Seventeenth", and there was more detail to it, saying: "That the people have a right to keep and bear arms; that a well regulated Militia composed of the body of the people trained to arms is the proper, natural and safe defence of a free State. That standing armies in time of peace are dangerous to liberty, and therefore ought to be avoided, as far as the circumstances and protection of the Community will admit; and that in all cases the military should be under strict subordination to and governed by the Civil power."

Here, again, the militia and the right to bear arms, are congruent, spaced by a semicolon, which is designed to coordinate a function between major sentence elements, but given equal position or rank, although they are too closely linked to be made into distinct individual sentences. Again, they are tied together, yet separated in a way.

# The Bedrock of the Second Amendment
# & its Application Today

The bedrock of the Second Amendment is found in the Glorious Revolution that occurred in 1688 on the British Isles. The Revolution began when influential Protestants thought King James II was attempting to suppress and potentially destroy the Protestant religion because of his stanch Catholic loyalty. As part of this extirpation, Protestants were said to be "disarmed" of their firearms. This fear led to an insurrection and the collapse of King James's regime as well as his exile.

Afterwards, William III and Mary II, James's daughter, took over the Monarchy, and created the English Bill of Rights of 1689 that restored "ancient rights", one of them being "the right" to have arms.

As the American Colonies grew larger, beginning with the establishment of a permanent colony in Jamestown, Virginia, in 1607, settlers required arms for hunting and protection, and were afforded the right to own firearms because of ancient rights, followed by the English Bill of Rights of 1689, which extended to the colonies.

When it came time for the American Colonies to separate themselves from the British, the colonists were heavily armed. The only way for the Redcoats to gain an advantage over the weaponized militias that existed in the Colonies was to seize hundreds of barrels of gunpowder in storage locations around the burgeoning America. Early on, the British had success, but the colonists considered this seizure of gunpowder as an act of war, and the Revolutionary War began.

Therefore, when the 13 original states unified to form the United States, the delegates called upon the lessons they learned from the War and British control, and required in their Constitution that ancient rights could not be taken from individual citizens by a central government. They also made it known that armed militias were necessary in order to maintain those individual rights if the Federal Government became tyrannous against them, as they felt the British Monarchy had become before the War.

Pragmatic minds certainly understand the original intent of the Constitution and the Bill of Rights, and it is why these rights are still in place and have been protected in one way or another by the Supreme Court for all these years. The question has become, though, whether or not the Second Amendment should be updated to align with the current state of the United States because of crime-riddled urban areas and high profile mass killings. Some people believe in the idea that the Constitution is dynamic and should be viewed as a "Living Constitution" with evolving interpretations that are contemporaneous with modern society.

The Supreme Court makes decisions based on their interpretation of the Constitution, but the Court does not amend the Constitution through their decisions. Changes to the constitution by amendment are proposed either by Congress through a two-thirds majority vote in both the House of Representatives and the Senate, or by a constitutional convention called by two-thirds of the State legislatures.

From 1789 to January 3, 2017, there have 11,699 proposed amendments, but only 27 of those propositions have actually led to amendments, and 10 of those came with the Bill of Rights. An example of a proposed amendment is Senator Barbara Boxer's proposal on November 15, 2016, to abolish the Electoral College and instead use the results of a direct popular election to decide the President of the United States. The proposal has gone nowhere like some many proposed amendments before it.

The last amendment to be ratified was the Twenty-Seventh Amendment, and it was submitted by Congress to the states for ratification in 1789, but it did not initially pass through. In 1992, nearly 203 years later, it finally became Constitutional law, prohibiting Congress from passing any legislation that would increase or decrease their current salary.

The process to amendment is difficult, and because of crippling political partisanship that is wrapped in party loyalty and polarized on a daily basis, any change to the Second Amendment will certainly have to develop when one party owns two-thirds of the votes in Congress.

The question by many today is whether the Second Amendment should be overturned or amended to deal with current issues of violence in the United States. Because the militia and gun ownership are bound by one amendment, the notion is complex. In essence, militias are designed to protect

Constitutional rights whether from the tyranny of the Federal Government or the invasion of a foreign entity, which makes it hard to say that militias are irrelevant in America's current age, or any age. Additionally, in order to have an effective militia, either organized or unorganized, firearms are required, but should everyone have the right to gun ownership or only militia members?

To curb violence in America, gun restrictions could provide some relief, but overturning the Second Amendment and taking guns from the public puts the entirety of the Constitution in danger for the reasons discussed. Unfortunately, the U.S. Federal Government in its current state does not provide a bi-partisan think tank capable of working together to solve the issues surrounding the country's violent culture, which is a complicated issue that is a tangle of matters that includes mental instability, poor education, oppression, varying ideologies, anti-nationalism, and yes, the easy accessibility of guns. All of these issues must be addressed and untangled to reduce violence in a systematic way.

# Photo Credits

Brady Campaign
David Skinner
National Archives
Jeff Kubina
Crimefilenews.com

Made in the USA
Monee, IL
11 December 2019